This book is for:

_____

From:

_____

On:

_____

I hope your friendship with Jesus keeps growing as you get to know him better.

Visit MyLifetree.com/Kids for more
fun, faith-building stuff for kids!

Notes From Jesus
What Your New Best Friend Wants You to Know

Copyright © 2018 Group Publishing, Inc./0000 0001 0362 4853
Lifetree™ is an imprint of Group Publishing, Inc.

Visit our website: **group.com**

Scripture quotations are taken from the Holy Bible, New Living Translation, copyright ©1996, 2004, 2007, 2013, 2015 by Tyndale House Foundation. Used by permission of Tyndale House Publishers, Inc., Carol Stream, Illinois 60188. All rights reserved.

Credits
Author: Mikal Keefer
Editors: Jody Brolsma and Jan Kershner
Chief Creative Officer: Joani Schultz
Art Director: Veronica Preston
Lead Designer: Jonny Vignola
Illustrator: Matt Wood
Assistant Editor: Becky Helzer

PRINT ISBN 978-1-4707-5029-9
EPUB ISBN 978-1-4707-5030-5

Printed in China.

009 CHINA 0721

10 9   25 24 23 22 21

~~~ Notes From ~~~
JESUS

What Your New Best Friend Wants You to Know

by
Mikal Keefer

LIFETREE

Group

TABLE OF CONTENTS

i WANT YOU TO KNOW...

Hi, friend!

You know my name, but I want you to *really* know me. Like I know you.

So let me tell you a few things about myself.

That's what you'll find in this book—stuff I'd like you to know about me. Because that's what friends do, right?

They meet and then they get to know each other better. They talk, laugh together, and pretty soon they're not just friends—they're *best* friends.

That's what I want for us. No matter how long we've been friends, we can always become better friends. I'd like that, and I think you'll like it, too.

So let's get started—right now.

Jesus

7

i WANT YOU TO KNOW...

▶ ▶ ▶ ▶ I love being with you.

You know how some mornings you wake up happy because you'll be with a special person that day?

Maybe a snuggle-close grandma is coming for a visit. Or you get to hang out with your best-ever buddy. Or maybe you and your mom are taking a bike ride together.

Well, that's how I feel when I'm with you. I'm always happy to see you. Always glad when we're together.

I like being with you. Did you know that? That I like being with you?

It's true, and I hope you feel the same way about me.

Let's have a great time together today...tomorrow...every day!

Here's how we can become even better friends...
We don't have to go anyplace special when we're together. Invite me to join you at school or when you're with your other friends. I want to be part of your everyday, all-the-time life. Let's do life together!

I LOVE YOU.

(FROM 1 JOHN 4:19)

Here's how we can become even better friends...
Let's tell each other *why* we love one another. I love you because of who you are, and I should know: I made you! Tell me why you love me. It will help you get to know me better.

10

i WANT YOU TO KNOW...

I like hearing you say you love me.

People talk to me—a *lot*.

Lots of times they pray, telling me what they want. That's okay—I like listening to my friends and giving good things to them.

But can I tell you something most people don't know?

As much as I like hearing what people need, there's something I like hearing even more. And I'll bet you like hearing it, too.

I like to hear, "Thank you."

I like to hear, "I'm glad you're my friend."

And most of all, I love to hear this: "I love you."

That's because I want to be in your heart, like you're in mine.

So in case you didn't know, I love you, too.

11

i WANT YOU TO KNOW...

I'm not surprised when you mess up.

I know you sometimes do bad things. Think mean thoughts. And sometimes you're selfish and disobedient.

I know that's true about you because it's true about everyone.

When you do something wrong, please talk with me about it.

If you're truly sorry, I'll forgive you. And I'll go with you when you try to make things right with other people. When you say "I'm sorry" to that friend whose feelings you hurt. Or you return something you took that wasn't yours to take.

As we become closer friends, you'll grow to be more like me. More patient, kind, caring, and forgiving.

But you'll still mess up sometimes. And I'll still be your friend when you do. Because I'm not your friend only when things go well. I'm your friend *all* the time.

Here's how we can become even better friends...
When I say you can ask for forgiveness, I mean it. If there's something you've done that makes you feel guilty, tell me about it now. You can trust me—I won't tell anyone else.

"IF WE CONFESS OUR SINS TO HIM, HE IS FAITHFUL AND JUST TO FORGIVE US."

(1 JOHN 1:9)

13

ANYONE

WHO HAS SEEN **ME**

HAS SEEN THE **FATHER!**

(JOHN 14:9)

i WANT YOU TO KNOW...

I'm just like you—but different.

It's sort of hard to understand: I'm a human being like you, but I'm also God. That might be confusing, but don't worry—I'll explain it all when we're together in heaven someday.

Here's what I want you to remember about me now: I was once a kid like you. I had friends. I went to school. My mom gave me chores to do and I helped my dad in the carpenter shop. You can imagine me whacking my thumb with a hammer.

But I never sinned. I never disappointed my heavenly Father.

That means I understand what you're going through when a friend's mean to you. When school is hard. When there's a fight in your family.

I get it—and I'm here for you. Come to me when you're sad or confused.

You'll be coming to someone who understands.

Here's how we can become even better friends...

Most people, when they think about me, imagine me as a baby in a manger or as a grown-up. But today I want you to think of me as a kid who's your age. What would you say to me if you met me when I was your age?

15

I know it's hard when you can't see me.

Your other friends come over to hang out. But me—I'm invisible. That may make it hard to remember I'm there and that I care.

But I *am* there. If you've decided to follow me, I'm closer than any of your other friends. They live down the block but, through my Holy Spirit, I live *in* you. And every minute of every day, I'm at work in you and around you.

When you feel moved to help someone, that's me.

When you see love in the world, I'm behind that.

And when you feel peace even when things are hard...yup, that's me.

I'll help you remember and believe, but you've got to do your part, too. You've got to look for me. Believe in me. Listen for my voice.

Because I'm there.

Here's how we can become even better friends...

The next time you pray, sit facing an empty chair. Imagine I'm in the chair, listening to you. I *am* listening, you know. I hear every word.

16

"BLESSED ARE THOSE WHO BELIEVE ▶▶▶▶ WITHOUT ◀◀◀◀ SEEING ME."

(JOHN 20:29)

17

NEVER STOP PRAYING.

(1 THESSALONIANS 5:17)

Here's how we can become even better friends...
Find a new place to pray today—someplace you've never prayed
before. Settle in and then tell me why you picked that spot, and tell
me what's been fun for you lately.

i WANT YOU TO KNOW...

I don't care if you pray with your eyes open...

Or while you're riding a bike.

Or while you're cleaning your room.

Or while you're eating a sandwich.

Or while you're watching TV.

Or while you're in class, in church, or in the bathtub.

Or while you're pulling on your sneakers, brushing your teeth, doing homework, yawning yourself awake, or drifting off to sleep.

It's okay with me if you pray while you're weeding the garden, jumping off the high dive, mowing the grass, getting a haircut, walking the dog, making your bed, riding in the car, hopscotching across the playground, or climbing a tree.

You can pray anywhere, anytime, and I'm happy to talk with you.

The more we're together, the better I like it!

i WANT YOU TO KNOW...

You'll find me in the Bible—all over the Bible.

I'm there—and not just in the first four books of the New Testament.

On the very first page of the Bible you'll see me helping create the world. And I'm there on the last page of the Bible in heaven with God.

I'm *everywhere* in the Bible!

That's because the Bible is the story of my love for you, and of God wanting a forever friendship with all of his creation.

Reading the Bible helps you understand my love. See how it looks and feels.

BIBLE

And you'll learn about yourself, too. You'll discover how I made you and how to have the best life ever!

If you don't have a Bible—one that's easy to read—ask for one.

Then start reading the book of John. It's packed full of adventure, truth, and excitement.

And best of all—it's full of me!

i HAVE HiDDEN YOUR WORD iN MY HEART.

(PSALM 119:11)

Here's how we can become even better friends...
Get comfortable and read the book of John for five minutes today. Before you start reading, pray to know me better. I'll help direct you to a spot in the book of John that shines light on me so we can become even better friends!

MAY GOD FILL YOU COMPLETELY WITH JOY AND PEACE. (FROM ROMANS 15:13)

22

We can laugh together.

When did I get a reputation as a sourpuss?

You hardly ever see a painting of me laughing or a stained-glass window that shows me giggling at a joke. I'm always shown serious and frowning, like I just sucked on a lemon.

But that's not me. Around me, there's light and laughter and joy.

The joy of being forgiven. The joy of feeling understood. The joy of fresh hope. In my kingdom, joy's an everyday event, sort of like our weather.

So it's okay if you and I aren't always frowning in concentration. Let's laugh instead. Let's be thankful. Let's dance and sing.

When something wacky happens to you, I want to hear about it. Tell me about what surprises you, delights you, and tickles your funny bone.

Let's laugh together!

Here's how we can become even better friends...

Do this: Tell me a joke. Your corniest, craziest, knee-slapper of a pun or your best-ever knock-knock joke. Let's laugh, friend!

23

I won't always give you ~~~ ▶▶▶ what you ask for.

It's true: I made everything, and I can do anything.

But I love you too much to always give you what you ask for.

Sometimes friends are friends only because of what they do for one another. Maybe you know someone like that—the person is your friend, but only as long as you help him with homework. Or share your lunch. Or make him feel smart or funny.

But our friendship's different.

I'm your friend because I love you. And I want you to be my friend for the same reason—because you love me, not because I can do things for you.

Besides, sometimes you ask for things that can hurt you or that can get between you and me.

So trust me that I want what's best for you.

And that I say "yes" as often as I can.

" HE HEARS US **WHENEVER** WE `ASK` FOR **ANYTHING** THAT PLEASES HIM. "

►►►► (1 JOHN 5:14)

Here's how we can become even better friends...
It's okay to ask me for things just as long as you know that you won't always hear "yes." So tell me: What would you like me to do in your life? Tell me, and tell how that will help you and me become even better friends. Because that's what I *really* care about.

i WANT YOU TO KNOW...

I don't just love you—I *like* you, too.

People talk a lot about how much I love them. And I *do* love them, just like I love you. It's because I love you that I came to earth to die on a cross so your sins can be forgiven.

That's *real* love, you know: laying down your life for someone.

But don't miss this: I *like* you, too.

I know everything about you, and I still choose you to be my friend. That's right—I know the things you don't want anyone to know. All your secrets.

I know them—all of them—and I still pick you to be my friend. I like who you are and who you're becoming.

And I *really* like knowing that you like me, too.

Here's how we can become even better friends...

Because I know you and *still* love and like you, we don't need to keep things from one another. You can tell me anything and I won't get mad or leave. So let's be honest with each other. Tell me what's *really* going on.

" THERE IS NO GREATER LOVE THAN TO LAY DOWN ONE'S LIFE FOR ONE'S FRIENDS. " (JOHN 15:13)

27

KEEP ON ASKING

...AND SEEKING

...AND KNOCKING.

(FROM MATTHEW 7:7)

28

I'll never get tired of your questions.

I love how you're curious. Curious about who you are. Who I am. How you fit into the world. About what's coming next for you.

We're on a journey together. How much fun is *that*?

I hope you'll keep asking questions because there's so much I want you to know. But mostly I just like that you come to me with your questions. I like knowing what you're thinking, and I love helping you find answers. So keep asking...and seeking... and knocking on my door with your questions.

But please know you won't always get answers. There are some things you'll have to take on faith—trusting that I'm here and that I love you.

So stay curious. Stay faithful. And please be willing to answer when *I* have a question for *you*.

Here's how we can become even better friends...
What are you curious about? Tell me so we can talk about it. And here's something that I'm curious about: What are you afraid of? Tell me about how that scares you—and how I can help you with it.

You can trust me.

Have you ever had a friend who's happy to see you one minute and then a grouch the next minute? Well, that's not me.

I'm the same from day to day. From year to year. Through all time. I'm always loving, always caring, always ready to keep my promises. That means you can trust me. Even if everything else you count on is falling apart, you can trust me.

If I tell you I'll do it, I'll do it. If I say I mean it, I mean it. You can take me at my word and know that I'll never, ever lie to you.

I'm here for you. Trust me.

I'M THE SAME YESTERDAY, TODAY, AND **FOREVER.**

(FROM HEBREWS 13:8)

Here's how we can become even better friends...

Everyone says, "You can trust me!" But they don't all mean it. Do this: Find someone who's known me a long time—maybe a parent, a pastor, or a friend. Ask, "How has Jesus shown that he can be trusted?" Listen to the stories they share. You'll see.

i WANT YOU TO KNOW...

I want you to meet my other friends.

When we became friends you joined a family—*my* family! You've got a whole bunch of brothers and sisters—they're all the people who love me. It would be great if you could meet them.

Some of those people have things to teach you about following me. They can help you have a rock-solid faith and show you how to take the next steps in getting to know me better. And you can help them, too.

As you're around my other friends you'll see how you can serve them. Bless them. Encourage them to grow stronger in their friendship with me. You're all in this together, you know. You're all walking with me, all discovering more about me.

So find some of my friends and introduce yourself. Tell them I sent you!

Here's how we can become even better friends..
Find a few of my other friends and ask them about me. Ask what they like most about me and how I've helped them. Listen to their stories. And share your stories with them, too.

WHEN YOU'RE WITH MY FRIENDS,

I'M
THERE,
TOO.

(FROM MATTHEW 18:20)

WITH ME, YOU'RE SAFE.
(FROM PROVERBS 18:10)

34

i WANT YOU TO KNOW...

I've got your back.

Friends can stick close when times get hard. Well, *some* friends stick close. Others disappear when bullies show up. When you have problems at school. When you're sad because your family is fighting.

I'm a friend who sticks with you. No matter what.

I'll help you solve the tough stuff. And when there's nothing you can do to fix a problem, I'll stay with you as you go through it. You can call on me anytime, day or night. I'll listen...because I love you. There's nothing you can say or do that will make me turn my back on you.

When hard times come, I'm with you.

I'm not going anywhere.

I've got your back.

Here's how we can become even better friends...

Feeling safe is wonderful, isn't it? When you and I are friends, you're safe. When troubles come, you won't be alone. You'll have me. Tell me: In what ways don't you feel safe today? Let's talk about that.

I'm your cheerleader.

A friend doesn't get jealous when things go well for you. A friend pats you on the back and cheers you on. A friend is happy for you.

That's me.

I'm your biggest cheerleader. I want you to do well. Even more, I want you to do *good*—to live a life that shows you and I are friends. A life that reminds people you're becoming more like me every day. That means you might not always get to be in the spotlight, because you'll be serving someone else. You might not win races, because you've stopped to help people who slipped get back on their feet.

That's okay. You're doing well. You're doing *good*. I'll be there to applaud and encourage you. I'm happy for you!

Here's how we can become even better friends...
Tell me about a jealous person you know. It might be a friend, a family member, or even you. What would change if that person cheered others on instead of being jealous of them?

I'LL BE YOUR GUIDE.

(FROM PSALM 32:8)

Here's how we can become even better friends...

Let's talk about you. What do you want to do when you grow up? Any ideas what might be fun? Let your imagination loose. Where do you see yourself as you go through next week? Next year? Next whenever? Tell me—I love hearing you dream.

i WANT YOU TO KNOW...

We both want what's best for you.

Of *course* you want what's best for you. Nobody sits around wishing the wheels would fall off her life. Nobody wants his day to land plop-slop in the gutter.

But here's the thing: I know what's truly best for you. You might think it'd be great if you found a zillion dollars. But I know that much money would ruin you. You might want a motorcycle, but *I* remember what *you* forgot: You can't drive!

So I'm asking you to trust me. To go with *my* plan, not yours.

Because I want only what's best for you—and that's to be my friend. To follow me. To let me guide your life.

That leads you to eternal life, and nothing's better for you than that!

i WANT YOU TO KNOW...

I love hearing you speak up for me.

I speak up for you, you know. I tell my heavenly Father, "That one? That's a friend of mine. I'm so proud of that one."

I'd like you to be proud of me, too. To introduce me to your other friends. To speak up and let people know you love me.

Because there are lots of people who haven't heard about me. Or they've heard, but they don't really know me. Not the way you know me.

I'd like to meet them, too. So, would you introduce us?

I love them, too, and want us all to be friends. I want to do for them what I'm doing for you.

Here's how we can become even better friends...

What would you say if you were to introduce me to your friends? Let's practice. Tell me—out loud.

11

YOU'RE MY MASTERPIECE!

(FROM EPHESIANS 2:10)

12

i WANT YOU TO KNOW...

I made you for a purpose.

You're not an accident. Or a mistake. You're who you are, where you are, because I put you there on purpose.

You're one of a kind.

Nobody else in all the world laughs quite like you laugh. Nobody else has your blend of skills, hopes, and dreams. Nobody else sees the world quite like you see it. I have so many things I want you to do. There are so many adventures waiting for you.

And only *you* can do them. Because I made you just like you are on purpose.

And I did a *wonderful* job, if I do say so myself.

Here's how we can become even better friends...

I know I did a great job making you. But do *you* know that? Maybe people say things that make you feel less than wonderful. Do this for me: Tell me what I did really, really well when I made you. And then thank me. And you're welcome!

I WANT YOU TO KNOW...

You're worth more than anything else.

Do you know how much I think you're worth? I can tell you—exactly. You're worth my life. You're worth the pain of dying on a cross. I did that so we could be friends and you could be with me forever.

The stars in the sky? I made them—but I didn't die for them. All the gold and diamonds hiding in the hills? I made them—but they weren't worth my dying for them. Nothing I've made was worth the cross except for you. You and the rest of the people I love.

So don't let anyone tell you you're not special. You are. You're special to me.

Don't let anyone tell you that you're unworthy. You *are* worthy, because you're worth everything to me.

Here's how we can become even better friends..

It's easy for my voice to get drowned out by other voices. It's easy to forget that I love you more than life itself. More than anything else in the entire universe. Read my note above out loud. Make sure you hear it and that my words sink deeply into your heart.

I LOVE YOU MORE THAN ANY- THING.

(FROM JOHN 3:16)

WHEN MY FRIENDS GET ALONG, PEOPLE KNOW THEY LOVE ME.

(FROM JOHN 17:20-23)

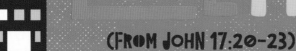

46

i WANT YOU TO KNOW...

My friends don't always agree.

Even people who love each other don't always agree. Maybe that's true in your family. It's definitely true in mine! In my family of friends, people sometimes argue. Their feelings get hurt. They disagree when it's time to make a decision.

That's one reason there are so many different churches.

Some of my friends decide to talk with me in one way, and some talk to me in other ways. Some decide to meet in buildings, and some meet in houses—or not at all. Some decide to get together on Sundays, and some get together on other days.

They don't all agree, but guess what? I love them all—every single one of them. I'd like them to get along, but I'll keep loving them—and you—no matter what.

Here's how we can become even better friends...

Even friends like us will disagree sometimes. I may ask you to do something and you'll decide, nope! When we disagree, let's talk about it. Let's not let disagreements push us apart. You okay with that?

Our friendship is getting some help.

Because I'm God, I'm not like anyone else you know. I'm not like your friends at school. Or like your family. Or even like people you meet at church.

That's why I asked the Holy Spirit—also called the Helper—to be part of our friendship. To come to you and live *in* you, if you've given yourself to me. The Holy Spirit will help you know me better.

By opening your eyes to how I'm working in and through you.

By opening your ears to know my voice when I speak to you.

By opening your heart to love me even more.

So get to know the Holy Spirit—the Spirit is your friend, too. I know and love you both, and I'm sure you'll get along!

Here's how we can become even better friends...
Even with the Holy Spirit's help, to know me better takes time. So do this: As you brush your teeth, tell me about your day. As you rinse your toothbrush, share anything you want washed from your life, anything you want me to forgive. We'll sparkle together!

THE
HOLY
SPIRIT
WILL
LEAD YOU INTO ALL TRUTH.

(FROM JOHN 14:16-17)

11

Not everyone's happy that we're friends.

Maybe you've heard of Satan. He isn't happy we're friends because he wants to push us apart. He wants to keep you from loving me and growing in friendship.

Let's not let that happen.

Here's how to keep Satan from chipping away at our friendship: Tell him to go away, and then draw close to me. I have *way* more power than he does, so when you're with me, you're safe.

When you turn to me, you turn away from Satan. And like most liars and bullies do, he'll leave you alone. So let's decide right now: We're in this together. Forever. There's no room for Satan to wiggle in between us.

It's you and me—and all the rest of my friends—from now on.

Here's how we can become even better friends...
Sometimes my friends are afraid of Satan. He can be scary, but here's something you'll be glad to know: *I've already beaten him.* He can't hurt me, and he can't hurt friends who cling to me. You're safe so long as you're with me. Tell me how that feels—I'd love to hear.

"RESIST THE DEVIL, and HE WILL FLEE FROM YOU."

(JAMES 4:7)

"

i AM
— THE —
WAY,
— THE —
TRUTH,
AND THE
LIFE.

"

(JOHN 14:6)

i WANT YOU TO KNOW...

Not everything you hear about me is true.

Some people think I'm just a guy who gave good advice. Advice like "do good," "be nice," and "don't get angry." They think I'm like those advice-givers on TV. But they're wrong. I'm not like *anyone* else.

Here's how I'm different: I don't just point *at* the truth, I *am* the Truth. I don't just give advice, I give life itself. And I didn't come to star on a TV show, I came to die for your sins.

You see, my goal isn't to make your life better. It's to make your life *holy*—and that's *better* than "better"!

So when someone says I'm like every other wise advice-giver, they're wrong. And they don't know me like you know me, or they'd know why.

Here's how we can become even better friends...

Do you think of me as a nice guy who loves kids (I am and I do), or do you think of me as something more? I *am* more, you know. I'm the way, the truth, and the life, and no one comes to the Father except through me. Is that how you think of me? Why or why not?

You'll hear from me in *lots* of ways.

Friends stay in touch lots of ways. Friends may call you. Text you. Show up at your door or send an email. Maybe even sneak up behind you and scream "BOO!" at the top of their lungs.

Well, I'm like that, too—I come see you in lots of ways. (Except for the sneaking-up-behind-you way—although sometimes I *might* surprise you.) You may hear from me in a thought that turns you in my direction. In a wise word from a pastor, a parent, or a friend. Or I may reach out to you from the pages of your Bible.

The Bible's my story, a *true* story I want you to know.

Not because you need to learn lots of Bible facts or because you get extra points for Bible reading, but because I want you to know me.

Just like I know you.

54

THE BIBLE IS TRUE

—and TEACHES US WHAT'S TRUE.

(FROM 2 TIMOTHY 3:16)

Here's how we can become even better friends...

I'm so glad your story is one we're writing together! But I still want to hear it. So would you share with me what's been a fun part of your story lately—and what's been a not-so-fun part?

"DON'T BE FAITHLESS ANY LONGER. BELIEVE!"
(JOHN 20:27)

i WANT YOU TO KNOW...

It's okay to have questions about me.

Even grown-ups have questions. And I mean *lots* of questions. About who I am. What I do or don't do. About when I'm coming back. There will be things about me that make you scratch your head and say, "I don't get that." All of my friends do that.

So if you have questions, that's okay. I won't get mad. I promise. I never get angry when my friends have honest questions and they listen to my answers and believe me.

So, ask. Really. That's what friends do—they ask, they listen, and they learn new things about one another. And sometimes they're okay with a little mystery in the friendship.

And we're friends, right? Right!

Here's how we can become even better friends...

What questions do you have about me? You can ask grown-ups who've known me a long time, but ask me, too. Listen for my answers—and believe what you hear!

I'm saving you a spot in heaven.

Some friends are your friends until they move away. Or they go to a different school. Then they sort of forget about you.

But you and me—we're friends forever.

Someday you'll join me in heaven. It's a beautiful place, and you'll fit right in.

But our forever friendship isn't waiting for heaven, because we're friends now. Today, tomorrow—we'll be friends from now on.

And here's something special about our friendship: You'll never outgrow me. There's always more to learn about me, always more I want to do with you.

As you grow, our friendship will grow.

And then, one day, we'll live together in the nicest neighborhood ever: heaven!

Here's how we can become even better friends...

It's fun sometimes to think about where you'll go on vacation. Well, let's think together about heaven—a place you'll have lots of time to be with me. Read Revelation 21:4 in the Bible (it's at the end), and then tell me what you think of joining me there.

THERE WILL BE NO MORE CRYING OR PAIN.

(FROM REVELATION 21:4)

MORE NOTES FROM JESUS

The Bible is just one way I can help you, encourage you, and remind you of my love for you. But it's a big, big book! So here are a few places in the Bible to look when you need to hear from me. As you read the Bible, maybe you'll find other parts that really stand out to you. Places where you hear my voice.

Go ahead and add them to these pages!

LOOK HERE WHEN YOU FEEL...

Angry

Proverbs 15:1
"A gentle answer deflects anger, but harsh words make tempers flare."

Colossians 3:8-10
"But now is the time to get rid of anger, rage, malicious behavior, slander, and dirty language. Don't lie to each other, for you have stripped off your old sinful nature and all its wicked deeds. Put on your new nature, and be renewed as you learn to know your Creator and become like him."

Lonely

Joshua 1:9

"This is my command—be strong and courageous! Do not be afraid or discouraged. For the Lord your God is with you wherever you go."

Psalm 139:1-6

"O Lord, you have examined my heart and know everything about me. You know when I sit down or stand up. You know my thoughts even when I'm far away. You see me when I travel and when I rest at home. You know everything I do. You know what I am going to say even before I say it, Lord. You go before me and follow me. You place your hand of blessing on my head. Such knowledge is too wonderful for me, too great for me to understand!"

Tempted

Galatians 6:1

"Dear brothers and sisters, if another believer is overcome by some sin, you who are godly should gently and humbly help that person back onto the right path. And be careful not to fall into the same temptation yourself."

Ephesians 6:11-12

"Put on all of God's armor so that you will be able to stand firm against all strategies of the devil. For we are not fighting against flesh-and-blood enemies, but against evil rulers and authorities of the unseen world, against mighty powers in this dark world, and against evil spirits in the heavenly places."

LOOK HERE WHEN YOU NEED...

Encouragement

Matthew 11:28

"Then Jesus said, 'Come to me all of you who are weary and carry heavy burdens, and I will give you rest.' "

Romans 8:28

"And we know that God causes everything to work together for the good of those who love God and are called according to his purpose for them."

Philippians 4:6-7

"Don't worry about anything; instead, pray about everything. Tell God what you need, and thank him for all he has done. Then you will experience God's peace, which exceeds anything we can understand. His peace will guard your hearts and minds as you live in Christ Jesus."

Forgiveness

Luke 15:10

"In the same way, there is joy in the presence of God's angels when even one sinner repents."

John 3:17-18

"God sent his Son into the world not to judge the world, but to save the world through him. There is no judgment against anyone who believes in him. But anyone who does not believe in him has already been judged for not believing in God's one and only Son."

Forgiveness (continued)

1 John 1:9
"But if we confess our sins to him, he is faithful and just to forgive us our sins and to cleanse us from all wickedness."

Help

Psalm 23
"The Lord is my shepherd; I have all that I need. He lets me rest in green meadows; he leads me beside peaceful streams. He renews my strength. He guides me along right paths, bringing honor to his name. Even when I walk through the darkest valley, I will not be afraid, for you are close beside me. Your rod and your staff protect and comfort me. You prepare a feast for me in the presence of my enemies. You honor me by anointing my head with oil. My cup overflows with blessings. Surely your goodness and unfailing love will pursue me all the days of my life, and I will live in the house of the Lord forever."

Psalm 121:1-2
"I look up to the mountains—does my help come from there? My help comes from the Lord, who made heaven and earth!"

Isaiah 41:10
"Don't be afraid, for I am with you. Don't be discouraged, for I am your God. I will strengthen you and help you. I will hold you up with my victorious right hand."

DRAW A PICTURE OF YOU AND ME

Remember, I'm always with you. I'm right beside you. I love you.